INSULT
to the
BRAIN

ESSENTIAL POETS SERIES 262

Guernica Editions Inc. acknowledges the support
of the Canada Council for the Arts and the Ontario Arts Council.
The Ontario Arts Council is an agency of the Government of Ontario.
We acknowledge the financial support of the Government of Canada.

NICOLA VULPE

INSULT
to the
BRAIN

AN ALTOGETHER UNRELIABLE ACCOUNT
OF MY CONVERSATIONS WITH POETS,
MOSTLY ABOUT DYING, BUT ALSO ABOUT
OTHER MATTERS GREAT AND TRIVIAL

GUERNICA
EDITIONS
TORONTO • BUFFALO • LANCASTER (U.K.)
2019

Elana Wolff, editor
Michael Mirolla, general editor
Cover and interior design: Rafael Chimicatti
Cover art: *Abstract Black #17* by Leonor Vulpe Albari
Guernica Editions Inc.
1569 Heritage Way, Oakville, (ON), Canada L6M 2Z7
2250 Military Road, Tonawanda, N.Y. 14150-6000 U.S.A.
www.guernicaeditions.com

Distributors:
University of Toronto Press Distribution,
5201 Dufferin Street, Toronto (ON), Canada M3H 5T8
Gazelle Book Services, White Cross Mills
High Town, Lancaster LA1 4XS U.K.

First edition.
Printed in Canada.

Legal Deposit – First Quarter
Library of Congress Catalog Card Number: 2018963020
Library and Archives Canada Cataloguing in Publication
Vulpe, Nicola, 1954-, author
Insult to the brain : an altogether unreliable account of my
conversations with poets, mostly about dying, but also about other
matters great and trivial / Nicola Vulpe.

(Essential poets series ; 262)
Poems.
ISBN 978-1-77183-376-9 (softcover)

I. Title.

PS8593.U 5I57 2019   C811'.54   C2018-906354-8

Contents

Frères humains qui après nous vives
—François Villon

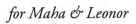

for Maha & Leonor

Not *If,* but *When*

We all will die. There is no escaping it. Even if we believe in an afterlife, Heaven or Hell or something in between, to reach that place we must pass through death. We are born, and we die. Whatever else may separate us: race, religion, nationality, gender, wealth, poverty, politics – all the usual differences, natural and contrived – these two events we all hold in common. Knowledge of death is what makes us human, unique it seems on this planet. Bees sacrifice themselves to protect the colony; the octopus starves herself into nothingness to ensure her young will survive; dogs are loving and loyal; jays not only remember where they have hidden food, but return to move it if they suspect someone else may know about the cache; chimpanzees make tools to collect ants for dinner. But as far as we know only we humans try to cheat death, to deny it its truth.

I am quite convinced that we try to cheat death; I am less convinced that we truly believe we will die. On this question, religion and art appear to be at odds with science, philosophy, literature and – yes – also art. Everywhere we dig up the remains of ancient peoples, from the pyramids of Egypt to the Siberian kurgans and the red ochre graves of Newfoundland, we find evidence that, whatever else they may or may not have believed, these peoples were not ready to admit the finality of death. For all their discord and animosity concerning details, religions do seem to agree that death is not the end. Whether we pass through the gates of death to eternal torment for our sins, pick up a snowy robe and golden harp and settle into our reserved seating beneath the throne of The Lord, or cross a desert to drink of the River Lethe before returning to this world to begin again, we get a second chance. Burdened as we are by our acute and imperfect consciousness of time, nothingness and the infinite, and the overwhelming evidence before us, we invented eternity and the great, creaking – and wonderful – edifice that is every religion and its promises.

On the other side of the scale, almost as an incidental effect of its investigations into how the world is constructed and how it moves, science heaps on the evidence: not only that we as individuals will die, not only that just as humanity was not always here and will soon be gone, but that the planet we call home, the sun it circles and the stars beyond, that in fact everything we know and imagine will, eventually, end. That this end is unimaginably distant puts the question outside the realm of practical problems requiring immediate attention; we have some five billion years at least before our sun begins to sputter. But distance does not alter the outcome. Just as each of our lives will end, so too will end our world, our sun, the galaxy and the rest of the universe – at least as we know them. Either the universe will complete its expansion and collapse back upon itself into nothingness or another universe, or it will continue expanding until every star or remnant of star is alone in absolute darkness, so distant from every other star that light from the one will never reach the other. The one or the other, equally the end.

And poetry? I have nothing earth-shattering to add, no particular understanding or insight. Since its beginnings, poetry has been, I think, very much about that other dimension that is also the domain of religion, about what it means to be human, and, often, though perhaps rather obliquely, about how we might behave if we are to be human. What, poetry asks, do we do with the brief time we have?

I began work on this small book some dozen years ago. I had got hold of a collection of poems by Nichita Stănescu, *Occupational Sickness*, translated by Oana Avasilichioaei. In her introduction Avasilichioaei describes the poet's last moments:

> While trying to revive him, the doctor asked him if he could breathe. He answered: "I breathe." Then, he died.

I know very little about death. In this I am fortunate. Some years ago I saw my mother die, and when I first wrote this introduction I was waiting for my father to die. I have lost a few friends, but only a few. In a world where parents still see their children murdered before their eyes, or watch them die because they have nothing to feed them, or no medicine to cure them, I am fortunate. My mother was old; she had come to the end of her life. My father also had reached his end.

I know very little about death, but it seemed to me that the manner in which Stănescu ended just about said it all: We breathe, then we don't. We are, then we are not. Of course, being a writer by trade or by affliction I couldn't leave it at that. I wrote a poem, "I Breathe," cribbed from Avasilichioaei's description. Then I wrote another, "Three Witnesses," about the death of Attila József, a poet to whom I have been greatly attached ever since, when I was 17 or 18, late in the night with rather too much wine in us I sat with my father on the stairs of his enormous empty house overlooking Narragansett Bay and he introduced me to this great and tragic poet. Destitute and alone, in 1937 at the age of 32, somewhere unpronounceable, József threw himself under a train.

My purpose in putting together this book is, of course, "artistic" or "poetic," in that for whatever personal reasons, whatever demons I mean to confront, I have wanted to write poems about poets and about how they died, which means also poems about how they lived and what they wrote. What better context in which to practice my craft than immersed in the lives and words of the poets I most admire – or detest.

But why poets, rather than, say, painters, novelists or violinists? Or for that matter, bricklayers, bakers, chartered accountants, pastry chefs, or computer programmers, politicians or drug dealers? For one, politicians excluded, poets tend to be rather noisier than the others. They write, they break the ice for a conversation and, being now mostly dead, are conveniently unable to contradict whatever I choose to say to or about them. If they are well-known, they are only relatively well-known; that is, perhaps known to those who at some time in their lives have turned to poetry for inspiration or succour, and briefly known to students of literature until such time as said students graduate. Which means that about poets I can pretty well write what I want. To most, it will all be news.

Writing what I want to write, and writing it well are altogether different matters, though. When I began this project I attempted to describe how poets died; that is, as best I could describe the physical circumstances of their deaths: Stănescu at the hospital, József throwing himself under a train, Alden Nowlan stubbornly walking to meet his end. Such descriptions in themselves make rather thin poetry, of course, and of course it was impossible to write about these events without engaging the poetry and the poets themselves. Thus, if the poems in this collection began all about how poets died, they became also, I think, about their lives and, especially, their poetry. This should surprise no one.

What might surprise some, though, is my choice of poets. I imagine every reader who picks up this book almost immediately riffling through it looking for a favourite poet. Where's Eliot? Where's Saint-Denys Garneau? Why are there no Chinese or Indonesian or Ojibwe poets? Why Trakl and not Rilke? And who are Husein Javid and Juan Geuer? I would be the first to agree. If a poet is missing, and most are missing, for the last century or so has produced far more poets that the handful I have written about here, the fault lies first of all with my ignorance. The only Ojibwe poet whose work I know is Armand Garnet Ruffo, and that, poorly, and of Chinese or Indonesian poetry I know even less.

Hence, the first of four criteria for inclusion: I must have heard of the poet. Second, the poet must have died, or at least been born. Though the project is about how poets die, I limited myself to poets of the last 100 years, approximately, which coincides neatly with the beginning (though not the end) of what Eric Hobsbawm called *the short twentieth century*, that century born in the slaughter of the Great War. A few of the poets I have included are not yet dead, but they all soon will be.

Third, I must have found something about the poetry, or the poet that made me want to write about him or about her. The poet need not be in anyone's canon, or famous. Hence, a poem about Ylli Dervishi, an Albanian poet I learned of through his obituary: He came to Canada to make a new life and was killed in a traffic accident. Hence, a poem about Husein Javid, cribbed from his daughter's account of how he was carted off into Stalin's gulag. Hence, a poem about Tal al-Mallouhi, a girl who at 17 posted some poems about freedom on a blog and was therefore promptly arrested. Hence, a poem about Juan Geuer, a brilliant sculptor, but also a poet – and a friend, who died a few years ago. For months I had a copy of my little novella, *Pia H.*, on my desk for him. I gave it to his widow.

Fourth, and this was the most difficult part, I think, I had to write the poem and, to my mind at least, it had to be worthwhile; and a month later, a year later, it still had to be worthwhile. There was a poem, for instance, about Diane Brebner. There were in fact many poems about Diane Brebner, how she beat cancer, and how cancer evened the score. But, as did so many others, these poems failed, or rather, I failed them and, therefore, banished them along with so much else I have attempted in my life to the depths of that last circle, the one from which there is no resurrection.

Intent

Suicide or accident?
The biographers can't agree,
self-inflicted certainly,
but what was his intent?

What had he meant,
dark as a lantern after a wedding,
with his pharmacy and his needles,
his books and his pen?

GEORG TRAKL
Salzburg, 1887 – Kraków, 1914 (cocaine overdose)

On Skyros – the Beautiful Boy

A square of earth,
a square beyond the sea –
Rupert's buried here.

A wee bit of England –
though nothing's green, just stones,
grey olive trees, a fence, and bones.

Rupert's buried here –
a square of earth, the sun,
goats that bleat and dream of rain.

RUPERT BROOKE
Rugby, England, 1887 – near Skyros, Aegean Sea, 1915 (septicaemia)

Gare de Rouen, 1916

Thus ends a world,
in a rush, overreaching,
suddenly.

Beneath the indifferent steel
of a first class carriage.

ÉMILE VERHAEREN
Sint-Amands, Belgium, 1855 – Rouen, France, 1916 (fell under a train)

Detail at War's End

It was over, and everyone knew it,
the beast about to die.

There did remain details, booty for the haggling:
a crook on a map, a signpost,
broken chimneys, the ribs of a church –

Your ruin, my ruin, hamlets with names like angels:
Sainte-Marie-aux-Chênes, Danne-et-Quatre-Vents,
                                        Saint-Avold.
Your mud, my mud. Your graves, mine – Wilfred

who went out one last time, as ordered.

WILFRED OWEN
Ostwestry, England, 1893 – Sambre-Oise Canal, France, 1918 (in action)

... With the Fever Set In

... with the fever set in, he knows. The city
unsure of sleep, the city certain only
of its bridges, of the slow river beneath,
the sky gathering. A wind
sweeps aside the sun. The city
indeterminate, he knows.

Lamps blink in their glasses, the boulevards
suddenly sparkle. The east
already dark. The river, like love,
here and not here, and yet here still,
the river and its bridges, the dead

GUILLAUME APOLLINAIRE
Rome, 1880 – Paris, 1918 (war wound & influenza)

Gumilev's Difficulty with a Tram

Rickety benches, soot-smeared windows,
woolly frost scratched off with fingernails.
Its number had disappeared, but it was yellow and red.

And it clanked and clattered,
and lurched as a good tram should,
so he wasn't concerned in the least,
he took out a newspaper and read.

The tram passed the theatre, a café he frequented,
fashionable houses where his friends usually met,
their curtains now drawn against the night chill.

A Paris waiter came aboard, lard stain on his vest,
an Ethiopian leading a giraffe, a painted elephant –
And the boulevard had seemed so empty!

How they all got on, he never said.
The tram hadn't stopped, it careened ahead
past dank workshops, a tavern, sod huts.

And still there were more. An antelope,
ostriches, bargemen and South Sea sailors,
a flock of Kirov ballerinas, a basket full of heads.

Some tram! he thought, and folded his paper.

Two men now, very business-like, very officious,
a briefcase full of papers, a soldier following.
Leave your things, they said.

NIKOLAI GUMILEV
Kronstadt, 1886 – Kovalevsky Forest, Russia, 1921 (executed)

In the Land Where the Moon

In the land where the moon
    in summer rolls fat across the fields
    breaking everything before it.

In this land with the crickets gone silent,
    and no one to hear, the yellow apples drop.

Here where the sea rises slowly like mist,   ·
    an overstuffed tom sleeps on a sill,
    his ribs trembling as he purrs.

In this land, beyond the black window
    snowflakes kiss the grey sea.

And she in her bed coughs
    and clutches in her fist the moon,
    red, grown thin as a knife.

EDITH SÖDERGRAN
St. Petersburg, 1892 – Raivola, Finland, 1923 (tuberculosis)

Behold, the Man

That scowling colossus towering over boulevards and squares,

that iron genius standing guard before libraries,
> before theatres and schools
> and academies of young fools in uniform,

that new god astride his plinth,
> love in one fist, revolution in the other.

> I deny it, I deny it all!

Not bronze, not steel or stone,
not granite, not marble.

Not chiselled, nor poured in a foundry,
not born of a hammer crack and flame.

> Tall as a lamp post, I admit.

Hands of a woodcutter, yes.
Lungs of a deep-sea diver,
I'll out-shout anyone in any theatre or square
from Novgorod to Novosibirsk.

> Guilty!

But a giant? A titan, a hero?

I died like other men,
an April morning of a broken heart.

I am a whisper,
a half-remembered murmur, a tremor.

I am a cloud, the hem of a cloud, the thread of the hem,
the worm that unwinds the thread.

VLADIMIR MAYAKOVSKY
Baghdati, Russian Empire, 1893 – Moscow, 1930 (suicide)

Flight from the *Orizaba*

He swam strongly at first,
though not as well, we thought,
as such a young man might.
It was difficult to know,
we high on the ship,
he in the warm sea below.
It was difficult to know
if he was swimming away
or reaching for a rope.
We did see him turn,
and a sailor swears he saw him wave.
It was, after all,
only ten miles to the coast,
and he swam strongly,
though only at first.

HART CRANE
Garrettsville, Ohio, 1899 – Gulf of Mexico, 1932 (drowned)

In Alexandria

Look: torsos and noseless busts,
a handful of worn coins under glass.
Here, the gods grew old.

They gather, a week's stubble on their cheeks,
in slippers and shirtsleeves, to sip sweet tea
and toss dice across a table, or smack down dominoes.
They puff at old-fashioned cigarettes in yellow paper.

A greasy fan turns overhead.

Their exclamations, no one understands anymore,
when one or the other turns a cataracted eye inwards and sees
how he bent over his oar at Salamis,
how he stood beside his shield, naked, at Thermopylae

and here, as the sun sets, measures the earth,
throws into the sky: names for the unnumbered stars.

CONSTANTINE CAVAFY
Alexandria, 1863 – 1933 (laryngeal cancer)

Poet by a Window, with Flowers

At the Montreal Museum of Art
we took our tickets and stood in line to see,
on the last day of the year but one,
among the whores, the soldiers
and otherwise worn-out men,
the occasional financier, beside a window
a tall man in a frame, friend to the painter.

He wears an ill-fitted suit, brown shoes, a green tie.
He needs a haircut, this tall man in his frame
with his collar frayed.

His long, crooked hands do nothing.
There's a tired white rose in a vase on a chair.

Beyond the window, the sky: red and yellow and grey,
and some sort of church the colour of old bronze,
but he doesn't see it.

He is posing for his friend, the painter,
and he is tired, he is hungry, though mostly he is cold,
and his broken shoes, his ill-fitted suit,
his unstylish hair and his tie,
the old coat beside the rose in its vase on the chair are no help.

Rumour says only one book remains,
somewhere in some library in Berlin, or perhaps Vienna,
twenty-nine poems of unfashionable innocence.

This discounts of course
the great sheaf he has hidden in his coat – just look!
And the ashes he threw out that shivering window,
here at the Montreal Museum of Art,
on the last day of the year but one.

Iwar von Lücken
Wiesbaden, Germany, 1874 – Paris, 1935? (starvation?)

Just Me, Fernando

Ricardo no longer writes.
His final letter was posted from Saõ Luís.
I set out tomorrow, he wrote,
the great brown river, the towering forest await.

I sent Álvaro to sea again.
On an Orient-bound tramp
he pecks at a bright new Underwood,
a treatise on the metaphysics of something or other.

In a fortnight he'll disembark at Yokohama harbour,
he will not return.

Do you remember that blonde boy?
The one we quarrelled over in Glasgow?
Mud swallowed him at Ypres.

And Bernardo, you with your great, rambling book,
and Vicente, António, Thomas, Raphael.
Jean Seul, who came home with me,
arm in arm from Durban.

It's years since we spoke.

Alberto, our master, has gone back to his sheep.
To hell with you all! To hell with you!
Poseur! was his final word to me.

And Ophélia?
Ophélia, forgive me,
I was born an old man.

FERNANDO PESSOA
Lisbon, 1888 – 1935 (cirrhosis)

De Falla at the Police Station

Don Manuel, with all due respect,
these are rumours, and rumours as you know
are usually lies.

Things are confused, the country's a mess,
but leave that to us, Don Manuel,
we'll fix things up in a snap.

No one's been arrested,
no one's been shot.
Certainly not your friend –
Federico you said his name was?

You may file a complaint if you like,
but sometimes a man just decides, Don Manuel,
not to come home.

And politics, Don Manuel,
is a dangerous indulgence
for a poet
or,
with all due respect,
even a musician.

Federico García Lorca
Fuente Vaqueros, Spain, 1898 – Granada, 1936 (assassinated)

Three Witnesses

There were three witnesses:
the station master, a travelling salesman,
the village lunatic.

The young man had been polite enough,
rather ordinary, thin.

A little threadbare,
interjected a ticket collector,
who in fact had seen nothing at all.

The station lights had been on for over an hour,
noted the stationmaster, who was formal
and stuck to the facts.

I was smoking a cigarette,
I was sitting there, said the salesman,
and pointed with his newspaper.

I looked at my watch, precisely,
confirmed the station master,
when the locomotive came into view.

But no one heard him,
or noticed that, to be precise,
his watch ran four minutes late.

Alone on the quay, the lunatic
described to a blue dog and an owl
how the ragged young man

had spoken with angels.

Attila József
Budapest, 1905 – Balatonszárszó, 1937 (suicide)

The Poet and Aviator
Expresses His Regrets to Il Duce

Mussolini? For dinner?

No, Maroni. No.
Tell him we flew to Vienna.
Tell him about the poems,
how we shoved them by the fistful into the sky!

And where were the women when we returned?
Where was Helen,
she who launched a thousand ships?

Maroni, do you remember?

In all of Greece, in all that blessed country,
not a woman who wasn't old or ugly,
not a whore to be got.

Mussolini?
Tell him I'm tired.

GABRIELE D'ANNUNZIO
Pescara, Abruzzo, 1863 – Gardone Riviera, 1938 (stroke)

Friend, Take From Me This War

Friend, take from me this war,
this war, its victors and the defeated.

Friend, take from me this burden.

I have chosen, and I did not want to choose.
Take from me the burden that I am a man.

Friend, give me a prophet who promises nothing,
a prophet who asks only that I live.

Like a cow in the field, a lizard on his stone,
that I know neither yesterday nor tomorrow.

Like a seabird pushed by the clouds, the mute stars.

Friend, a prophet who asks only that I breathe,
and cares nothing of the end.

César Vallejo
Santiago de Chuco, Peru, 1892 – Paris, 1938 (malaria)

Osip's Birthday

Someone suddenly remembered:
It's Osip's birthday. Where's Osip?

And we all stopped what we were doing,
we put down our glasses,
we swallowed our food and wiped our mouths.

That's true, we thought,
it's Osip's birthday. It's Osip's birthday
and we don't know where he is.

The light bulb above the table went yellow,
grease stains appeared on the wallpaper,
the host cursed the floorboards, the architect and the builder
who obliged him to put folded papers under three table legs
just so our drinks wouldn't tumble onto the carpet.

We looked at each other, our eyes asking the same question.

Until the one who'd remembered stood,
stood and raised his glass: To Osip! he said.
And we answered together: To Osip!

But the wine was sharp,
the dumplings soggy,
and the herring too salted.

Because on his birthday,
everyone knew where Osip was.

Osip Mandelstam
Warsaw, 1891 – transit camp, Soviet Far East, 1938 (deported)

Tell Them

If ever they should ask, tell them this:

Tell them Irina died in an orphanage,
there was nothing to eat.

Tell them we left, we slipped away where we could:
Berlin, Prague, Paris –

We disembarked with our cardboard suitcases,
our useless currencies.

As hungry as lice,
and as welcome.

Yes, if ever they should enquire,
if ever they should trouble themselves to ask –

Tell them I came home.
Tell them it was winter.

Marina Tsvetaeva
Moscow, 1892 – Yelabuga, Tatarstan, 1941 (suicide)

The Neighbour

When I woke that morning
I couldn't find my father.

They had come in the night
and searched every room,
even the kitchen,
but they didn't search the room where I slept.

While they searched, my father smoked –
a pack and a half, my mother remembered.

The NKVD man smoked too,
he reached into my father's pocket
and took two cigarettes.

When they left with him
they took his passport,
his birth certificate,
five notebooks, his letters,
23 photographs,
115 books in Arabic, Turkish and Persian,
and a wicker basket full of manuscripts.

We'll never know what my father had written.

I don't need to remember these things,
we still have the receipt,
and the order for my father's arrest.

It has three signatures:
Parshin, an official,
Pavlov from the NKVD,
and Verdiyev, our neighbour.

HUSEIN JAVID
Nakhchivan, Azerbaijan, 1882 – Shevchenko, Siberia, 1941 (deported)

Rehabilitation

We brought the session quickly to order.
Everyone, it seemed, had somewhere urgent to get to.

We heard from the family, their lawyers,
historians, representatives of the old order,
the Church, which (surprisingly) had no opinion.
But there really wasn't much we could undo.

He was dead, after all, dead like all the others.
Dead, Miguel Hernández Gilabert.
And though it had been years and years,
his file remained a troublesome matter.

So we agreed on one or two poems in schoolbooks,
a few streets in the far suburbs.
One day, we promised the family (off the record),
we would do better.

But his was still a troublesome matter,
there really was little we could undo.
And, anyway, everyone
had somewhere urgent to get to.

MIGUEL HERNÁNDEZ
Orihuela, Valencia, Spain, 1910 – Alicante, Spain, 1942 (tuberculosis)

The Executioner Presents the Facts,
as He Remembers Them

We lined them up in a brickyard,
it was 1944, it was over.

We had one cigarette for the lot,
Take a minute, I said.

One of them had a notebook,
I remember the notebook.

Take it, he said to me. Poems, he said.
What would I do with poems? I answered.

It's over, we're beaten, I said,
I'll be lucky myself to see Christmas.

Miklós Radnóti
Budapest, 1909 – Abda, Hungary, 1944 (executed)

Only His Glasses

It's a story, that poem, an invention,
a last scrap of light.

So often I have dreamt ... it begins.

But it wasn't like that, Youki, it wasn't.

There were only his glasses, Youki,
which now I send to you.

ROBERT DESNOS
Paris, 1900 – Terezín, Czechoslovakia, 1945 (deported, typhus)

Revolutionary, Unrepentant

The first came stillborn,
the second was indentured.
The third went to prison.
The fourth and the fifth were twins,
they went east into the taiga
and were not heard of again.
The sixth tried to make amends for the third,
and became a policeman.
The last joined the anarchists,
and wrote poems.

The first was buried in a bit of cloth,
the second fell lame and was hungry.
The third found employment
breaking fingers and hands.
Rivers cut the taiga and the steppe,
at every crossing a boatman waits for his coin.
The sixth was meticulous,
and rose through the ranks on merit.
And the last?
The last was beaten and deported.

The first had no name,
and hence cannot be remembered.
The second sat on a snow covered hill,
he looked down at the bright city,
the tiny lights, the stars above,
and decided to sleep.
The third fell mysteriously ill
and took weeks to expire.

Of the fourth and the fifth
I have spoken already.
The wind hisses across the water,
the boatman pulls at his oars.
The sixth was assassinated
at the height of his career,
in the flower of his years –
a young girl from the mountains,
with a smile, a white ankle and a knife.

And the last?

A stone without words
marks the shore where he'd stood, penniless,
waiting for the boatman.

VICTOR SERGE
Brussels, 1890 – Mexico City, 1947 (cardiac arrest)

You Wake

You have seen death,
your eyes are opened.

Your lip tastes of sweat and road-dust,
your feet have swollen in your boots,
you shrug your shoulders.

Wise Ulysses, beyond the river of forgetting.

The sun warms the wheat and the orchards,
the city below grows distant, beyond the dark river.
You trudge on into the cold, green hills

where, maybe, there is a woman,
a woman who may have said, Yes.
Yes, my love, this will be our hearth.

CESARE PAVESE
Santo Stefano Belbo, Italy, 1908 – Turin, 1950 (suicide)

The Indifferent Luck of the Poet

There's some luck in stopping
to straighten a tie, in missing a tram.

I saw them afterwards, I saw the pink shapes in the river,
I heard a girl whimper as the skin fell from her arms.

I suppose that's what luck means. I too was wounded,
but as you can see, it was trivial, an interesting
and masculine scar, appropriate for a movie hero who,
naturally, lives to tell his story, and the story,
more important, of that girl by the river.

We all come back to that, don't we?
Every morning at 8:15 precisely.
It was my fate to straighten my tie,
it was my fate to miss the tram.

My fate that tonight the surgeons
have set down their instruments.

TOGE SANKICHI
Osaka, 1917 – Hiroshima, 1953 (failed surgery)

Insult to the Brain

November 9th,
New York, St. Vincent's, of:

Insult to the brain, that is to say,
ACTH, a cortisone-type drug,
eighteen straight whiskeys, or so he claimed,
amphetamines, or so it is rumoured,
morphine, also a rumour,
forty Cornish pints in an afternoon, unsubstantiated,
women naked under their mackintoshes, confirmed,
Caitlin, also confirmed,
purloined shirts,
pointless lies,
written and unwritten,
an unfinished novel,
an unmade bed,
pneumonia,

an unkept appointment with Stravinsky.

DYLAN THOMAS
Swansea, Wales, 1914 – New York City, 1953 (alcohol, etc.)

Havana, Across the Sea

Havana was only across the sea, unreachable
as some distant star. We stopped, and turned
and watched the waves, and believed we saw,
despite the moon, her muted lights. They gave
the horizon shape, they formed the night around us.
That part was true, Mr. Stevens, exactly as you said.
A boy, I walked along the sand you spoke about,
I saw the hermit crabs wave their long antennae in the night,
I saw them climb the mangrove roots, and fall,
while in the town, beyond the bridge, a jukebox
carved from wilderness a yellow dome of song.

Why, Mr. Stevens, is it said you called a priest?
What was it in that place and time that frightened you?
There was no order there, I think. Nor its opposite,
nor any thing we could construe would make us drown.
The crabs, the tepid sea, wavelets that lapped the shore,
far Havana, farther stars. In the town that jukebox in that bar,
a drunk nursing a broken hand. And on a stool, Hemingway,
or his ghost, back from Idaho to bid us all farewell.

WALLACE STEVENS
Reading, Pennsylvania, 1879 – Hartford, 1955 (stomach cancer)

Galileo, In These Times

In these times of extreme lassitude,
standing on the subway platform
we ruminate once more on the details of our dismissal:
all the usual things, the stock markets mostly.

On TVs above us, the ticker ribbon:
boys in a far place fling homemade bombs at tanks,
women run for the border. Someone important
is meeting someone else, also important.

We know we're being watched.
We play a game, grinning and waving at the cameras,
marking a point when one adjusts itself,
turns its eye to follow us up the stairs.

Bug-headed policemen have closed ranks.
They've brought out the fire hoses and the gas.
But that's in another country, another city,
down another street.

We walk home in our worn shoes,
another month unemployed,
and wonder again how it was your *Galileo*
angered us so in our indifferent youth.

Bertolt Brecht
Augsburg, Germany, 1898 – East Berlin, 1956 (cardiac arrest)

Trieste

We were warned about the wind.
You'll be swept into the stones, or worse.
They put ropes across the great square. Hold on!

The flags, mostly red and green,
registered hardly a quiver.

We were warned about the heat.
July, we were told. August!

At sundown we sat on the long quay,
the sky was still, immaculate, pink.
And the water so very pleasant around our feet.

What kind of city, this? we asked.
Who does it belong to?

No one, came the answer.
Everyone. Itself.

But, listen. Be wary of Opicina, the cliffs.

UMBERTO SABA
Trieste, 1883 – Gorizia, Italy, 1959 (heart failure?)

Everything

So much for Mexico, the black dogs
and their dreamless sleep.
So much for the bare-assed monkeys
scampering across the savannah,
the silver spiders with their nests –
soft grey spheres soon to burst.

So much for things that swell and breathe,
things that grow small and die, objects
– a green chair, a door, a room and a radiator,
a vase with two daffodils – things
that faithless wives and philosophers
collaborate to diminish.

So much for GIs and Lucky Strikes and jeeps,
for hard-headed detectives in black and white,
Duke Ellington and all dreams American.
So much for the deserter who held on to his rifle.
So much for Indochina, the censors.
So much for your Swiss dancer, her body all triangles.

So much for meningitis and cancer,
for tasting the worms before they taste you.
So much for your Uncle Anatole or André,
the handy one who built an A-bomb in his back shed.
So much for Hollywood and rain on the Seine,
a heart with one half still.

BORIS VIAN
Ville d'Avray, France, 1920 – Paris, 1959 (cardiac arrest)

The Ancient Remedy

It's an ancient remedy, Sylvia: fall in love, marry.
Make children, settle for a Formica kitchen,
dinner parties and martinis, an oversized Buick, the lawn.

But somewhere under the earth, my dear,
a young woman lugs over tree roots and stones,
both hands on the handle, a red suitcase full of poems.

SYLVIA PLATH
Boston, 1932 – London, 1963 (suicide)

Shakespeare, Political Prisoner

I'd have thought, Nicolae, I'd have thought,
that after all these years you'd have let it go.

What shall I confess?

That I wrote poems? that I wrote sonnets?
that in this country not a country,
this pastiche drawn and redrawn in the corners of grand maps,

that in an old language,
a tired language, a language no one cares about,
I believed myself Shakespeare?

I surrendered my poems, one by one.
They fell like sparrows in November sleet.

Who but you, Nicolae, could have been fooled?

My village continues unidentifiable,
a suburb of a suburb of a suburb,
of a weary capital of singular unimportance.

My house with its red-tiled roof, its one cold-water faucet,
broken gate and worn lace curtains, was long ago removed.

Children play in a muddy courtyard,
their mothers shout from bare windows.

Nicolae, why send a man to prison?

The sun, eventually,
erases everything.

VASILE VOICULESCU
Pârscov, Romania, 1884 – Bucharest, 1963 (cancer)

Thursday, the Museum of Noble Causes

It is a museum,
as might be expected,
of corpses.

I inhabit here
a place of relative honour,
a room to myself,

though a small one
and in a far wing,
far from the paying throng,

a room that every Thursday,
when entrance is free,
fills with light.

Occasionally,
also on Thursdays,
someone comes to visit.

Already this year
there have been two,
broken-hearted students:

one boy, one girl, who
in a kinder world would have come
on the same Thursday.

Instead, he in Taksim Square,
she somewhere I've forgotten,
they'll be arrested.

As I was, long ago.
Though, being a notable of sorts,
I wasn't quite alone.

Committees were formed.
Articles were written.
Posters were printed and affixed
in locations of prominence
in all the important capitals,
and many lesser ones as well.

Luminaries spoke:
Sartre, Picasso, Robeson,
Simone de Beauvoir, Neruda,

all inmates like me now,
Neruda, for instance,
with his own, south-facing hall.

He is our friend, they said.
Save him, they said.
Save Nâzım Hikmet!

November, the lights of Istanbul like a necklace.

A freighter idles its engines,
a man climbs aboard, shivering.
Save Nâzım Hikmet!

Don't make me laugh!

You were unable to save even yourselves.
Our dreams fell to earth
like angels without wings.

It's Thursday again.
A heartbroken student, the girl,
has returned.

And I –
faded paper,
artefacts in glass cases,
a pair of pens,
a cup I've never seen or used,
old notebooks –

I can say nothing,
I cannot warn her.

NÂZIM HIKMET
Salonika, Ottoman Empire, 1902 – Moscow, 1963 (cardiac arrest)

Poet with Blue Truck

It was raining, or maybe it wasn't.
There was a rainbow over the river
and a blue truck –
or so someone remembered.

His publisher said it was suicide.
His friends suspected murder,
but could produce neither motive nor method –
or rather, too many.

Theories and counter-theories and conspiracies:
that redhead we'd not seen before nor since,
that man with the umbrella, unopened,
though it was raining – if it was raining.

Lucy, his wife, was living in Chicago, and didn't care.
He'd signed the divorce papers.
All she needed was for someone to shake off the dust
and drop them in the mail.
Which his mistress, also called Lucy,
was only too glad to do.

For their part, the police, acting on instructions from above,
settled on 'accident,' and wrote this in all the reports.

They had their reasons.
Book sales increased from nil to a few,
a major publisher in Germany bought rights,
another in America commissioned a biography,
which no one ever wrote.

As in all the mess that followed,
what with the tanks taking up positions in front
of the ministries,
the helicopters rattling overhead,
and the army and police working overtime.

The rain, the blue truck, the rainbow,
suicide, murder, an ordinary distraction –

No one could agree on anything,
save when they gathered him up from the boulevard,
the singular disappearance of his soul.

OMAR DE GROOT
Maastricht, Netherlands, 1930 – Buenos Aires, 1966 (unknown)

The Poet Descends, Willingly, the Stairs

My mother said:
A woman about to die,
her kiss is cold.

I answered, Mother,
I cannot do otherwise.

Not today, she said.
Go another day, go tomorrow.

Wait for spring, the New Year, she said.
Wait for the mountain storms to fall quiet.

Wait for the tulips to fill the valleys,
for the sun to warm your young face.

Mother, I whispered, I cannot do otherwise.
My lot is to go down the long stairs.

My lot is to descend
into the loneliness of the moon.

FOROUGH FARROKHZAD
Tehran, 1935 – 1967 (traffic accident)

Life Apologizes

I'm sorry, said Life,
who had never apologized to anyone before,
I should not have left you.

I look at your pictures, I look and remember.
Time turned around just to look at you!

Yes, you loved me too much – or so I thought.
You clung like a schoolgirl to wilted daisies after
                                        a country dance.

And who was I? A schoolboy fumbling at your breasts?
A soldier? A married man passing through town?
Whoever I was, I lied.

I promised you everything,
I promised to let you grow old in my arms.

HALINA POŚWIATOWSKA
Częstochowa, Poland, 1935 – Warsaw, 1967 (failed surgery)

Uncle Ho Attends the Fall of Saigon

Best be dead.
You got that right.

A tank's always got room
for one more ghost.

Sit wherever you like,
put your feet up, have a smoke.
Enjoy the parade.

You got that right.

Kick their asses:
De Gaulle, Kennedy, Johnson,
Nixon, Ford.

Then discreetly exit,
like a carnival conjurer,
or a saint.

Ho Chi Minh
Hoàng Trù, French Indochina, 1890 – Hanoi, 1969 (heart failure)

The Poet Bids Adieu to His Poems

You are, as we know, turtles.

The male has his moment,
and is indifferent.

The female fusses about in the sand,
and is gone.

The hatchlings are fully formed,
no metamorphosis, no second chance.

For the crippled and the unlucky,
under the shrieking gulls,

the sea is an infinity.

PAUL CELAN
Cernăuți, Romania, 1920 – Paris, 1970 (suicide)

Brush, Paper, Sword

Angels tumble,
gods slink into the earth.

Brush:
the sun crosses the sky,
the moon fades.

Paper:
clouds smother the stars,
the sky rains upon the sea.

Sword:
Fish yearn to be birds.

YUKIO MISHIMA
Tokyo, 1925 – 1970 (seppuku)

English Poets, Explained

The food's horrid, the weather worse.
It rains and rains, and rains some more.
Outside it's soggy, inside it's 1984.

Take Stevie, poor Stevie,
everything proper, no complaints.
She was trying and trying, she said.

She was swimming and swimming, she said,
the dark tow dragging, she said,
tired of lying.

STEVIE SMITH
Kingston upon Hull, England, 1902 – Devon, 1971 (brain tumour)

Dreamless

I awoke and there was nothing in my hands.
No marble head, its white curls, its dull, unseeing eyes,
the silent, stony lips – nothing.

How I would have wished for such a gift,
an old stone to weigh down my arms. A broken torso,
a spearhead, a greave or blade grown foamy with time,
a single coin struck by an obscure tyrant –
he ruled from his promontory a rock-strewn sea-lane.
A ragged bit of papyrus.

But no! I opened my eyes, and nothing.
Snow drifting onto the dark waves,
the sea stretching eastward into night.

GEORGE SEFERIS
Urla, Ottoman Empire, 1900 – Athens, 1971 (ulcer)

The Lip of the World

I came to the lip of the world.
Dull it was, loamy, nothing
like the glittering promise, nothing
like the vertiginous well, the fall.

It smelled of old clothes, of a house
where the dead had rested, nothing
like the year I turned twenty-nine,
the year I took the train to Paris,
nothing like those girls in April under the plane trees,
their neatly pressed blouses, their white arms.
Oh how their blue eyes smiled!

I came to the lip of the world,
a yellow ridge, brittle scrub,
broken shells, broken butterflies,
their colours littered across the stones.

GABRIEL FERRATER
Reus, Catalonia, 1922 – Sant Cugat del Vallès, Catalonia, 1972 (suicide)

This Night, I Drown No More

These, the fish pulled up from the dark,
their mouths suck at useless gas,
gills flair, fins and tails shudder.

Swim bladders burst.

Buenos Aires, Buenos Aires,
even your wind drowns us.

I am, we agreed, a single point.
A single point that is everything.
And, tonight, will be nothing.

ALEJANDRA PIZARNIK
Avellaneda, 1936 – Buenos Aires, 1972 (suicide)

Estadio Chile

In the stadium in Santiago de Chile,
the bleachers are empty, the crowds far away.
We sit on the pitch, our tongues
thick and slow, we dream of water.

In the stadium, like lovemaking,
no two encounters are exactly alike.
With which finger shall we begin?
Shall we be quick, and just do the knees?

We wait our turns in darkness,
whisper names and known fates.
If ever …
Tell Violeta … Tell Carmen …

No, just say good-bye …

Víctor Jara
Lonquén, Chile, 1932 – Santiago de Chile, 1973 (executed)

In Brutus' Shadow

We saw then – do you remember it?
we saw then the tyrant only,
nothing of Cassius, nothing of vanity,
ambition. Nothing of the stars, defeat.

We sided then. Do you remember it?
We sided with Brutus, his honour, certainties,
the heavy instruction books of History,
Hegel, Marx, Gramsci and, of course, Neruda.

Sad verses, broken hearts, sand,
time's stony teeth, shipwrecked dreams.
Saint Neruda. Do you remember him?
Blood's spattered on his shoes as well.

PABLO NERUDA
Parral, Chile, 1904 – Santiago de Chile, 1973 (disputed)

Lads

The masks of death are infinite.
Some are modern, a wrecked car on the night road to Milan.
Others ancient and more deliberate: drowning,
a knife to the throat in the bath.

It was about the boys, the lads.
That, at least, was what the press said.

The lads, who in the alley behind a flea market
shine shoes and run shell games.

The lads, or so the press insisted,
who when they don't have their hand in your pocket or purse,
when they've had a drink, or at least a smoke,
draw up in Byzantine detail the ultimate bank job,
the airtight confidence trick.

The lads who know that one day, one day soon,
they'll deck themselves out in a silk suit and new shoes,
swagger into the casino at San Remo.

Lads who settle today for rolling a drunk or a queer,
who flip cards against the wall where they piss.

Lads who've already forgotten where their mothers live,
if it isn't after a particular run of bad luck
to borrow a few thousand, and maybe sit for a meal.

Lads who are known to the police,
who hang about the stony patches
that in this neighbourhood pass for piazzas,
who know by name those gentlemen who purr in on weekends
with their foreign cars and sweetish cologne.

Lads, the courts and the press would eventually establish,
who understand that in this world

either you get screwed, or you don't.
Even if it takes a switchblade and your fists.

PIER PAOLO PASOLINI
Bologna, 1922 – Rome, 1975 (murdered)

Transmigration, Perhaps

There are 99 ways to tell a story,
one for each name of God,
10^{14} – a thousand billion sonnets on 10 pages,
if only you pay minimal attention to meaning
and cut the paper right.

All science is a circle, and so are poems,
says Monsieur Queneau from behind his circular glasses,
while contemplating various body parts: his,
and young Marie wiping down his table,
the circulation of the blood in particular, the liver,
the slow levitation of bubbles in beer.

Hano, who circumnavigated Africa,
Magellan and Drake, who circled the globe
such are the states of being according to Pythagoras.

And since this is Monsieur Queneau,
circular glasses, cravat and slide-rule,
and this Paris, this a café,
there's a dog turd on the sidewalk outside.

The women in their pumps and heels don't miss a beat.

A small man, likely balding under his green hat,
button number two missing from his coat,
briefcase and newspaper, the kind with small print
that intellectuals read:

Monsieur Queneau, I try not to lie
at least not on Tuesdays and alternate Saturdays.
I deal in certainties.

There are 99 ways to tell a story,
something like that many names of God,
10^{14} sonnets, provided you cut the paper right,
and rain washes away dog turds.

But, Monsieur Queneau,
in the 40 years you've been dead. Or not dead,
I still haven't decided about poems, circles,
circumnavigation and science.
Or, indeed, what to do about this button on my coat.

RAYMOND QUENEAU
Le Havre, 1903 – Paris, 1976 (cancer)

You'll Do, Said Death

I've come for Brel, says Death, Jacques Brel.
That's not me, answers the man in the bed.

Are you sure? says Death.
Romain, says the man in the bed, Jules Romain.

Well, answers Death, I find that surprising.
This is October 9th, room 305, Bobigny:

Chestnut trees outside the window,
leaves bright yellow under the rain.

Not me, says the man in the bed,
that Brel you're looking for, Jacques Brel,

he went to the South Pacific, the Marquesas
he lives with a local girl, Madly,
and flies a plane to Ua-Pou.

It's all in the papers, everyone knows.

Yes it is, says Death,
pulling back the sheet and slipping into the bed.

Brel's a singer, says the man,
I've only one lung, and a half-rotted one at that.

So I'm told, says Death,
putting his arm around the man's shoulder.

Look at the chart! Read the name! cries the man.

That might fool the paparazzi, answers Death.

JACQUES BREL
Schaarbeek, Belgium, 1929 – Bobigny, France, 1978 (pulmonary embolism)

Not Both

Are you there, Djuna, are you alive?

That butch girl came by again, left roses in your mail,
the other, the sickly one too. Sat like a stray cat on your step,
sat until I shooed her away. And that foreign lady called.

Letters you won't read rot on the stairs,
the bottles at your door are piled four deep.

Hate us if you please, hate us like a lie hates the light.
But for God's sake, Djuna, for God's sake decide.
This world or the other, this or the other?

DJUNA BARNES
Storm King Mountain, 1892 – New York City, 1982 (not specified)

An Old Man Prepares to Doodle

An old man prepares to doodle
on the last page of a notebook.

A notebook that's been forgotten a few times
on tables of cheap cafés, once or twice in a streetcar,
dropped in the mud beside a field lying fallow.

A notebook that's been returned by kindly strangers,
a blonde kid who showed up in the middle of the night,
someone in Scotland who sent it back without a note,
in a stiff brown envelope, misaddressed.
Heaven knows how it got here!

A notebook that's been read by policemen with fat fingers,
policemen who stayed late
typing out reports on its perplexing contents.

A notebook held together by a blue rubber band,
a strip of brown paper on the spine,
a notebook so full it refuses to close.
Left on a table its pages riffle open like a fan.

Pages dark with ink and doodles,
Maori tattoos, long improbable words,
pages filled and overflowing, all but the last,
empty, where the old man,
once again in a tired café ponders

an arrow to the infinite.

Gyula Illyés
Rácegrespuszta, Hungary, 1902 – Budapest, 1983 (cancer)

I'm Walking

We're stubborn like that,
Maritimers.

Or just a touch too well planted
in this field we've been given to plough,
rocks and pine roots and all.

We'll give quarter.
It's the way we're made, I suppose,
but expect none.

And, like I told Yukio,
the Cancer Ward takes no prisoners.

So be it then.

So be it!

But there'll be no gurney,
not for Alden Nowlan of Desolation Creek, Nova Scotia,
lately of Fredericton.

I'm walking!

ALDEN NOWLAN
Stanley, Nova Scotia, 1933 – Fredericton, 1983 (emphysema & cancer)

I Breathe

I breathe, I whispered.

Indeed, he answered.
But what ails you?

I breathe, I repeated.

You have no fever, he said.
Our instruments register nothing unusual,
no untoward inflection.

Your humours remain unremarkable,
your heart ponderously normal.

I breathe, I said.

He hooked the stethoscope claws into his ears
and shoved the cold disc under my shirt.

Nothing, he said,
save perhaps that same worm
rasping at your liver.

I breathe, I called to him as from a tunnel.

Yes, yes, he answered,
and poked a hard, white light into my eyes.

I breathe, I shouted from somewhere
far, far away.

NICHITA STĂNESCU
Ploești, 1933 – Bucharest, 1983 (hepatitis)

Jump! Don't Jump!

Plod on, plod on, it's not so bad.
Mum managed it, so did Dad,
mornings drowned in mustard fog,
days an endless well. Nights like tar.
We were born, we'll die. What's the rush?
rope or razor, pills or high ledge –

Jump! Don't jump! It could be worse,
the grey-beige air, the limping clock,
that grinning idiot in the glass,
and the boozy truth, which is this:
The other side, it might be the same.
Plod on, plod on through the sucking muck.

Philip Larkin
Coventry, 1922 – Hull, 1985 (oesophageal cancer)

Man on Bridge

Did the falling man cry out?
That drunk who tumbled from the bridge?
No one heard. It was night.

No one heard if he obeyed the rules, the law of gravity,
if he splashed into the shivering river,
or soared off to join the saints, wingless above the city.

When I'm in Charlottetown next, Milton,
I'll stop by St. Pete's for a chat.

Then I'll get down
and tighten the screws on that satin-lined box of yours.

We can't have you back, shouting and crowing,
when finally we turn off the TVs and shut down our laptops,
when even the radio goes quiet.

When we notice it's been years since we closed our eyes,
stepped off the bridge, too late to decide
if we'll fly or meet the river.

MILTON ACORN
Charlottetown, 1923 – 1986 (heart disease & diabetes)

One Theory – or Another

We all have our theories.
Mine says suicide. Suicide and your mother.

Primo! Who's at the door?

Yes, we all have our theories.
Mine says an accident, vertigo, a stroke,
excess fluid in the left ear,
a vein under the skull suddenly stopped.

Primo! Why don't you answer me?

Mine says a catastrophic hallucination,
Poland, a prim uniform behind a table,
the attendant physician, a list.

Primo! Who's at the door?

Mine says water, yellow oil smeared on the landing.

Primo! Where are you?

Such is my theory.
A theory of everything,
a theory of bursting stars, galaxies fading,
infinite cold.

A theory of crumbling particles, electrons, fermions,
neutrinos suddenly gone, time shivering.

At the top of a stairwell in Turin,
a theory of nothing.

Primo?

Primo Levi
Turin, 1919 – 1987 (accident or suicide?)

Self-Portrait with Pines and Water

It was always about those trees, wasn't it,
Gwendolyn, the shuddering pines reflected?

No matter how bright the water,
eventually, we lose the sky.
Those cloud wisps lazing above the spires disappear,
we sink through water-soaked leaves,
foamy weeds tickle our pale feet.

They're heavy as iron now, your trees,
black and slippery under the towering water.

Long ago they tumbled from the rock face.
Maybe it was lightning, maybe it was wind,
maybe it was too much light, too far above,
the brown silt settling, the brown silt below.

GWENDOLYN MACEWEN
Toronto, 1941 – 1987 (alcoholism)

The Poet

Four known species,
distinguishable only *post mortem*:
light, dark, tedious, and bombast.

Ranges through all habitable climates,
with unconfirmed sightings
even in dankest Alabama
and the stone deserts of Arabia.

Easily provoked, given to posturing,
territorial.

But generally pleasant, of no practical use,
like a cat.

NICOLÁS GUILLÉN
Camagüey, Cuba, 1902 – Havana, 1989 (Parkinson's disease)

On an Island, the Guards Drunk or Snoring

On an island, the guards drunk or snoring,
he searches the stars, the silver sea.
In a far country on a bridge he watches the sleepy river,
dull blue, grey as the veins inside his elbow.
In a park he counts the green ducks on the pond,
only the green. Rain falls on café tables.
Tap-tip into the cups, tap-tip into saucers and ashtrays,
tap-tip, tap-tip, tap-tip.

Water beads up on a spider's web. She retreats
into a hole under the eaves, the web trembles in the wind.
On a bus to Thessaloniki, a woman with a parcel
folds her arms across her shaking breasts. On the island,
the guards still unseeing, a wave turns over a mottled stone.

YANNIS RITSOS
Monemvasia, Greece, 1909 – Athens, 1990 (not specified)

A Book, the Wind

In Genoa, it's no longer raining.
A priest in his cassock hurries,
a book tucked under his arm,
there on the mountain
at the edge of discovery.

A red ribbon flutters from the book's cover.
Best of Show, 1st Prize, it says in gold letters,
but in Italian.

Not his, not the priest's,
but Voronezhski's *Lirika*,
a book I've just invented –

The East wind,
not the South but the East,
teases the sea.

The ships are below us,
idle at their moorings.

The wind tugs at the cassock, at the ribbon,
the priest clutches the book

on whose pages somewhere
someone has noted in a margin:

In the cave in the mountain
at the centre of darkness
we seek only darkness.

ALESSANDRA VORONEZHSKI
Free Territory of Trieste, 1947 – Genoa, 1991? (unknown)

Auto-da-fé

… and those of us bereft of souls,
what if we are to Him invisible?
Our hour is short, we play it out
and go

In this hotel of reasonable comfort,
just the sort one would expect
for a cultural event of modest ambition,
in a town of no particular note or charm,
among the bones of an empire
fallen on hard times and doubt.

The telephones have gone dead,
the lights begin to flicker.

I slide open the window, the moon has not risen,
no stars tremble in the sky.
It is that hour when the wind dies,
that hour when everywhere in the world
lovers stroll, arm in arm,
and remember together scraps of old songs.

But not in Sivas, not tonight.
There'll be no lovers or old songs.

I look down from the empty sky
to the street and the boulevard beyond,
heaving rivers of hats and fists.

God hates you, God the merciful ... Hates you!
God the indulgent ... Hates you! God the forgiving ...
Hates you! God! God! God!

... will damn these souls we do not have

The men have found weapons,
a fire axe, kitchen knives.

One, I don't know him, has kerosene.
He's lined up bottles on a table,
fills them, stuffs their gullets with rags.

Much use they'll be, we'll be the first to burn.

On the top floor the women have crowded together.
Some say they'll jump.
It's just high enough, says one.

Others are more optimistic, they lean out the windows,
wave and call to the policemen,

who, far below, far down the street,
beyond the hats and the fists and the shouts,
lean on their cars and smoke.

METIN ALTIOK
Bergama, Turkey, 1940 – Ankara, 1993 (burned by mob)

Somewhere in the Papers,
Generals and Gentlemen

We read about it in the papers,
four column-inches, page A11.

One of those squalid little countries
where things always turn nasty,
Namibia or Niger, or maybe Nigeria.

In Africa anyway.

There had been a campaign of sorts,
he being a poet and environmentalist.
But of course no one listened,
not anyone who mattered.

Not the president and general,
whose name we'll not mention,
not the governor,
not the judge, the jailer,
not the sleepy soldier from the north,
who could have left the door open.

Under a thin rain in England
a wispy-haired gentleman wrung his hands.

Most unfortunate, he said.
It is not within our power, he said.
These are sovereign nations.

Though in the end
it was all very British, very proper:

By the neck until dead.

KEN SARO-WIWA
Bori, Nigeria, 1941 – Port Harcourt, Nigeria, 1995 (hanged)

The Sphinx of Gljúfrasteinn

When we arrived on the fell
it was raining, of course,
and there wasn't a sheep.
Can you believe it?
Not a sheep to be seen.

But there he was, as promised,
Halldór,
the grinning sphinx furiously writing,
as the rain turned to sleet,
the sleet to snow.

HALLDÓR LAXNESS
Reykjavik, 1902 – 1998 (consequences of Alzheimer's disease)

The Poet, T. H., Attempts His Obituary

A commoner's son, labourer,
lantern-jawed, Poet of the Realm,
a tower of friendship and daring,
Promethean.

In hospital, London,
of excessive Englishness,
and vocabulary.

TED HUGHES
Mytholmroyd, England 1930 – London, 1998 (cardiac arrest)

No Season for Dying

I don't want to die in spring. It's the season
for suicide. The office girls on Ste-Catherine
are never more beautiful, eternal. And an ordinary death,
an unshaven grub with tubes in his throat, what's that
to the ice dotting the black river, these girls in new shoes
stepping round snow and water on the sidewalk, laughing?

The cracked earth's impossible to cut, worse than winter.
In any case, no one's available for a funeral,
even the worms have gone. The others are at the cottage
or in Europe, the gravediggers are drinking,
couldn't be bothered. Cadavers stink, the river is far,
and the ghosts that inhabit them wither in the sun.

No season, this, for decision. Uncertain. The river
turns and bubbles, stupid against its stones. Everyone
speaks of the fat moon, fat and yellow and old,
but what of the sun? The sun grown thin, thin
and afraid. The empty trees reclaim their sky,
a sudden comet sweeping the stars.

I don't want to die during winter. Think of it:
A soul trekking across the snow, naked of course,
destination undisclosed, through the pine woods,
over the mossed stones, stumbling upon steaming rapids,
too cold to swim, nothing to do but turn back,
wait shivering while the world wanes, or plunge in.

MALCOLM JONES
Montreal, 1954 – Saint-Zénon, Québec, 1999 (traffic accident)

Arrival

We sailed in from somewhere south of Iceland.
Telegraph Hill threw out a shadow we could not see
                                        through the mist.

The ice-strewn gulf, the river. Tomorrow.

We carried in our trunks, beneath the carefully folded coat,
our shirts and thin trousers, the rubbish of our histories.

Heraclitus said this, Euripides that. Homer, of course,
Herodotus and Sappho, Plato's step-children.
                                        Archimedes. Voltaire.

We wore them like our skins, ill-fitting, chapped,
                                        supreme disguises.

We disembarked like everyone else, with these monsters,
                                                smiling,
a cloudless January morning, into the blazing cold.

Louis Dudek
Montreal, 1918 – 2001 (pernicious anaemia)

The Bench Opposite

I awake with a start. On the bench opposite,
a woman asleep, in her arms an infant.

I'm on a train, the landscape
clattering by all wrong, the trees
not real trees. Short, scrubby things.

Suddenly, a village. But the doors
on the houses not as doors should be,
and the roofs not proper roof colours.

On the window, a chipped sticker,
the international No Smoking symbol,
and something else, mysterious, also forbidden.

And a long explanation below,
in a language I've not seen before,
all vowels and diacritics. Footsteps.

In a cloud of foreign tobacco
the conductor steps in, says something,
presumably also all vowels and diacritics.

And the woman on the seat opposite, yawning,
points to those three tickets in my left hand.

Ken Smith
Rudston, England 1938 – London, 2003 (Legionnaire's disease)

327

The detectives have come of course,
three hundred twenty-seven of them,
a pair for every country,
including a few already under water,
and a few imaginary.

And the Vatican, of course,
which sent just one,
affording him particular dispensation.

There's no blood to see,
nothing anyone could construe as 'evidence,'
and no one is saying anything.

Not now, not ever.

But the detectives are not disappointed.
Some crimes are meant not to be solved,
and who but Bolaño could place a detective,
not just one, a half-dozen at least,
in a poem?

A nurse switches off whatever it was that was running,
no one really cares anymore.

Nicanor Parra continues his long trek
down that long corridor that is a country,
throwing soiled papers before him.

The stars blink at the enormous prints he leaves,
bathtubs in the desert,
filling with ocean and tears.

ROBERTO BOLAÑO
Santiago de Chile, 1953 – Barcelona, 2003 (liver failure)

Sewing Baskets

One girl sells God. From behind her cart
heaped with onions she calls to passers-by.
Another girl dreams. In forty days exactly
she will sing herself into the sky.

In this city girls don't call or sing,
they encipher their hearts in stolen notebooks,
which they hide at the bottom of sewing baskets.

A girl is buried –
not the one who dreams, her time is not done,
not the one who sells God, another,
who married, whose husband will be forgiven.

In this city, God is lazy, I suppose,
indifferent to who does what or where, incurious
of the secrets buried at the bottom of sewing baskets.

Nadia Anjuman
Herat, Afghanistan, 1980 – 2005 (murdered by husband)

A Large Man and His Shadow

He stands in full afternoon,
a rolled sheaf in his fist,
hatless.

Squinting,
he sways and he shouts
like a drunken man,
the chorus in a Greek tragedy.

Though there's no one about,
if we discount the dog asleep in the dust,
and the yellow worm lunching,
high above in the tree.

The words will not stop.

He passes his tongue over his lips,
raises that fist with the papers,
and wipes his forehead with his wrist.

Behind him his shadow,
true as the promise of night.

IRVING LAYTON
Târgu Neamţ, Romania, 1912 – Montreal, 2006 (Parkinson's disease)

A Poet Returns to His Unhappy Nation

Rumour has it, when you returned,
a holiday was spontaneously declared.
At eight in the morning students informed their teachers
that classes were cancelled, and headed for the airport
with copies of your books their parents had kept hidden.

In the outlying factories no one started up the lathes
                                              and the presses.
The workmen, and the women with their kerchiefs had
                                              gone into town,
and now stood about on the fashionable boulevards,
rubbing their raw hands, smoking and laughing.

Office workers crowded among them and chatted.
Boys and a few girls perched themselves on lamp posts
                                              and in trees.

Officially, nothing was planned. Your arrival was a non-event
orchestrated for a non-person, who was, in fact, not arriving.
A non-person who had not been warned by some official
                                              or other
that he would be arrested and who had not, therefore, fled
                                              to France
or arrived, later, in America with an invitation from FDR
                                              himself,
but no visa, or returned, only to at last be arrested.

That non-person who, between the beatings,
fed his fellow prisoners with poetry and philosophy,
and long afterwards settled, of all places, here.

And continued to write poems until such time as he could,
at a non-event such as the one that was now patently

not unfolding,

step down from an airplane and himself declare
his non-existence once and for all null and void.

But this was, even the police chief admitted, no longer

possible.

Ministers, the Mayor of the capital, even a former president,
under investigation for a number of vague offences

– everyone –

had the previous night been visited by the same ugly dream.

What if no one is there to greet him?
What if he came again, and became again a non-person?
Out of spite or, indifferently, out of habit?

I would be so ashamed, said the dream. And shame
is something we have worn far too long and well.

Thus a motorcade of gleaming Mercedes was hastily

assembled,

red and green and white bunting miraculously procured,
auxiliary police brought out to increase the circumstance,
but also and according to tradition to ensure the peace.

And we, left behind, once again in Toronto in February,
after so many years looking up at an empty apartment,
clutching this poem you'd left behind
about men who will die, and the moon.

GYÖRGY FALUDY
Budapest, 1910 – 2006 (not specified)

In the Night, a Tall Man

If only we could find the tall man,
the man who ran out across the snow.
He was in sneakers and a tee-shirt, no coat.

He just jumped from the truck, he ran
out there past the Shell station, between the houses.
But I didn't see much, it was dark, 5 a.m.

This says Mr. Bernard, Mr. Bernard,
who was fiddling with his radio, and looked up,
too late to see what actually happened.

He ran out across the snow,
but I was more worried about the others,
says Mr. Bernard,

who called 911,
who led Roza away from the car,
who went back for Ylli.

Who was too busy with the blood
to notice Ylli's eyes,
how quiet he was.

YLLI DERVISHI
Tiranë, 1958 – Toronto, 2007 (traffic accident)

An Uncertain Geometry

There is an uncertain geometry in these poems.
Plato, for all his bluster,
might just have approved.
Or, what is more likely,
adjusted ever so slightly
the strings on his master.
Socrates says …

Here the manuscripts are faulty,
or diverge. Confusions and lacunae
we must ourselves resolve.

If the soul can be described,
it is (indeed) like the universe and time, exactly,
with vectors. Or, failing calculus and sums,
in the white shelter between words.

MARGARET AVISON
Galt, Ontario, 1918 – Toronto, 2007 (not specified)

When Mahmoud Died

When Mahmoud died, everyone continued quarrelling.

A minister from the Authority nursing a hangover,
– don't ask why – suggested Jerusalem, which everyone knew
was of course impossible.

Beirut, said another. Bury him in Beirut.
He belongs to all Arabs!
Then why not Damascus? said someone else
whose intentions were not clear.

A young girl from the other side of the wall,
Gabi, her name was,
said she would refuse military service,
because Mahmoud was dead,
because she loved poetry.

A delegation from that same side agreed,
and respectfully asked to attend the service,
wherever it might eventually be.

They wished to pay their respects, they said.
We agree with Mahmoud, they said.
We have no right, us and our bulldozers.

But, as always,
no one could agree in precisely what capacity
they might participate,
and what formalities, if any, were required.

A group of French poets, mostly on the left,
proposed a cemetery in Paris.
He belongs to the world, they insisted,
so Paris is the natural choice.

And where were you in 1956? snapped someone in reply.
Behind cannons! Shouting at us from behind cannons!

Of course there were many who were angry,
in Tel Aviv especially,
but also in Toronto and Teheran, and a hundred other cities.

Though few could remember why.
Their parents, after all, and their grandparents,
like Mahmoud's, had long ago ceased to exist.

Yes, when Mahmoud died everyone continued quarrelling.

There were delegations from as far away as New Zealand,
and speeches, of course, and flowers,
and many notable events.

But no one thought to give to Mahmoud,
now that he was dead,
a stone or a bit of wood from that house he'd left as a boy,
a branch from that lemon grove he'd fled in the night.

MAHMOUD DARWISH
al-Birwa, Palestine, 1941 – Houston, Texas, 2008 (failed surgery)

Kant's Apocrita

The old philosopher on the quay
stands and waves. This green ship.

Dream the florid Indies, Cochin,
the Pacific's long, slow swell.
Disembark, your last, great work complete,
a monument. The red parrots of Peru.

Ah! homesick for the Baltic wind,
how colourless reason warps and frays.

Among the potatoes and the stones,
the forgotten cities, the frost,
beneath the pinprick stars, their seeping light,
the ants ate everything.

A crumbling page begins '… the preceding sentence
is of utmost importance,' and there ends.

For there, said someone,
not Juan, nor Kant himself,
is where Truth resides.

JUAN GEUER
Soest, Netherlands, 1917 – Ottawa, 2009 (stroke)

His Passing, Largely Unnoticed

His passing went largely unnoticed.
The death of a poet, after all,
rarely gives cause for comment.

Unless he garnered some large prize or other.
Unless he stood accused of unspeakable acts.

Or hailed from an unimportant country,
a country with few celebrities, no sports stars or tycoons,
insufficient generals.

A country that honours, for lack of better,
botanists, teachers, a virtuoso oboist.

And he was, near as anyone could tell,
an honourable man.

He made a point of refusing prizes.
Poetry has no colour, he said.

And his country, for all that he loved it,
has generals enough.

DENNIS BRUTUS
Salisbury, Southern Rhodesia, 1924 – Cape Town, 2009 (prostate cancer)

A Man Reading a Poem

Somewhere a man is reading a poem,
a poem about a man in a car,
a man in a car, beating a woman.

The man who is reading the poem
stands in a stadium at night.
He is wearing an expensive suit and a stylish cravat,
both somewhat out of fashion.

Women have brought notebooks,
those who forgot have found bits of paper.
They hope to get close to this man,
this man reading a poem.

They crowd around the stairs leading up to the stage,
they are smiling, but each is suspicious
and fearful of the other.

She might elbow her way to the front
to meet the man reading the poem
about the man in the car, this man
beating a woman.

Who is also, incidentally, wearing an expensive suit,
also somewhat dated, though no cravat.

This man who is tiring now,
whose knuckles are beginning to hurt,
who has opened his hand and begun slapping.

The man who is reading the poem finishes up,
he sips a little water, spilling some on the lectern.

Applause ripples through the stadium,
and the women in the stairs tense up for the assault
on the man who read the poem
about a man in a car, a man
beating a woman.

A woman who did not go to the stadium,
a woman who did not bring a notebook,
or bit of paper, or wait at the stairs,

a woman who stayed where she was,
where the man slapping threw her,
on the side of the road,
where she is unable even to dream

that the man who made the poem, the man who read
                                        the poem,
that the women with their notebooks and their bits of paper,
that all those people applauding

opened the door of the car,
and in their strong hands held the arm of that man,
who punched her until he was tired,
then fell to slapping.

ANDREI VOZNESENSKY
Moscow, 1933 – 2010 (stroke?)

Eclipse

Here's to us!

Here's to us,
who in a sudden moment of contemplation,
count.

Count back and count forward and notice:
how little is left.

Here's to us,
sifting through the dust and the blood,
like archaeologists or detectives.

We who try to reconstruct the catastrophe,
the instant the slide began.

Here's to us,
who in a sudden moment have known our fate,
bedsores and all.

We, who have seen the dark centre of the sun.

Who have seen our mothers die,
swimming in morphine.

G. C. Laugier
Saint-Céré, France, 1930 — Toronto, 2011 (consequences of vascular dementia)

We Are Left, Gliding Away

It's been a long ride, outer space,
longer even than evolution,
the creaking gap between the sludge
and that mammalian aberration
with a quill in his hand, Thomas Mann *et al.*,
longer even than the six days of creation,
and that seventh about which we know nothing.
The universe is expanding at a frantic pace.
So quickly, in fact, that the faster you travel
the further you are from the edge. Go figure.
It's not a journey for the faint of heart, for cynics or boors.
They'll stew themselves like winter cabbage
until the stench of their disillusions
seeps even into the wine.
They'll open an airlock and step into the void,
they'll look out across the light years, the millennia,
they'll infect stars and galaxies and black holes so distant
not even sorrow can reach them.
And still we shall be no nearer.
Which is why, I suppose,
you choose to stub out your last cigarette,
and leave us, gliding to our purpose.

WISŁAWA SZYMBORSKA
Prowent, Poland, 1923 – Kraków, 2012 (not specified)

The Judge Sends a Young Poet to the Gallows, Handing Responsibility to God

One must be diligent.

The enemy is at the gates,
he has amassed great armies, his ships and his rockets
on the plains and the seas around us.

He pays foolish young men
to set off bombs in pursuit of hopeless causes,
but in fact to advance his own vulgar interests.

One must be diligent.

Ours is an ancient nation, and sacred,
and its traditions must be upheld.
We prefer to keep things simple,
and you were, after all, arrested.

You are of the faith,
and therefore should know better.

You write with words not understood in the capital,
though they are in truth the words of the holy books.
These words you have abased to your worldly ends.

One must be diligent.

A high officer is jealous of your wife's beauty.

There are seven days in the week,
the sun rises and sets,
snow covers the mountains,
spring follows winter.

Birds fly and rain tumbles from the clouds,
spiders spin their silk, it is written,
and fish swim in the dark sea.

You are a man,
and God alone judges.

HASHEM SHAABANI
Ahwaz, Iran, 1982? – undisclosed prison, Iran, 2014 (hanged)

Woman at the Airport

This woman at the airport,
she's old, clearly.
She's 86, or maybe 85,
and blind.

She's been pulled from the line.
A policeman remembers his grandmother,
he brings her a chair,
and calls for tea.

But his instructions are formal.
Consider her dangerous!

The woman adjusts her scarf,
and places her hands on her lap.
The policeman stands beside her,
unsure where to place his hands.

Dare I tell you?
Dare I tell you, grandmother?

I was fifteen,
I heard you read just one quatrain, and since
I have loved no other.

Simin Behbahani
Tehran, 1927 – 2014 (heart failure)

Upside Down

Strange times, my dear,
the executioner's walked off the job.
The judge commuted the sentence to
whatever the prisoner chooses,
which is – can you believe it?
a marriage proposal to the prosecutor,
promptly accepted.

In distant Madagascar a dodo rose from the sand and sang,
though so far as we know these birds never sang before.

At home the news briefs were equally distressing,
the generals in their big hats and uniforms,
and the CEOs in theirs
concluded a suicide pact – after breakfast, of course.
The cleaners found the note in the afternoon.
Such regrets, it reads, such regrets.

The Queen and her minister, old
and accustomed to hedging, preferred exile.
The ship sailed off at midnight, a sickle-blade moon
unhooked from the cranes on the docks and followed her out.

The Wall Street boys checked themselves in to the loony bin,
they're out there on the lawn now,
rolling joints and giggling at the clouds
and the coloured bits they pulled from their phones.

Yes, yes, strange times,
the camp guards have forgotten their whips,
the secret policemen their wires
and dynamos and special chairs.
They've come to our school, and made no arrests,
they're digging flowerbeds and hanging their heads.
They brought geraniums and violets,
but the children prefer roses.

It was only the ad-men and the priests
who had their throats cut.
Their bodies still litter the foyers of the better hotels,
though in the interest of public health
the blood's been mopped up,
and velvet ropes set out to deter the curious.

My dear,
Guaraní have come down to Montevideo,
they've pulled their pirogues out of the estuary
and set up camp in a park. San Martín and Columbus
have traded their pigeons for laundry, a woman roasts a fish
and laughs. She's read, it seems, both Rousseau and Marx.

Strange times, my dear,
the landlord's dropped in for tea,
he brought back the rent, a chicken – and Turkish sweets.
My friend Michael's got his old job back,
he's fixing things that make other things work,
things supremely useful and fun.

Yes, the blacksmith's at his anvil
shaping ploughshares and scissors,
lovers frantic in the night know the night will not end.

And the milk of our sorrow tastes of cardamom and honey.

EDUARDO GALEANO
Montevideo, Uruguay, 1940 – 2015 (lung cancer)

When I Dream, I Dream the Sun

When I dream, I dream in bursts.
The other night I dreamt
blonde women with pink breasts
piling into bed with me.
Blessed man in sleep, you say.
But no! Bird-taloned and beaked,
they perched upon me in a row
and screeched.

Mr. Tranströmer, you said
we cannot dream the sun. I disagree.
I drank a glass of wine, I ate Roquefort,
the neurotoxins, it's been proved,
attack the cells. I saw the sky,
yellow as an egg. And in it,
high above the sea, a man,
tumbling.

TOMAS TRANSTRÖMER
Stockholm, 1931 – 2015 (unspecified illness)

Iceland, South Coast, Somewhere Unpronounceable

The sheep ignored us.

It had seemed so small, hardly a ribbon,
a trickle from the mountain lip,
and the speckled meadow, trivial.

We trudged on, the sheep ignored us.

We picked at last our way up,
over the moss-green boulders.

And, beneath the dark roar, turned again

to the bright valley from whence we'd come,
the mad, black giants beyond the road,
their feet in the wind-ragged sea.

My heart is broken.

This is where the world began, this:

Midnight, under a blue-washed sun,
a puffin slapped skyward.

Sigurður Pálsson
Skinnastaður, Iceland, 1948 – Reykjavik, 2017 (cancer)

Concerning What We Did in the Andes

We peered over the edge, the heights were,
as they say in novels, 'vertiginous.'
No echo, the wind, the sun too bright,
we squinted at the snow, the purple darkness below.

They dropped slowly at first, the words,
then fell away like stones from a crumbling wall,
uncoiled like ropes into the void.

We peered again. I kicked a pebble.
No echo, the wind, the sun.
We're done, I said, they're gone.
Words, anti-words, sentences, complex,
compound and simple, pronouncements,
explanations, equations, excuses,
lies, Lies, LIES!

Syllogisms into the purple darkness,
whatever silence it is that waits below,
the endless kelp that washes,
dull streamers in the icy green.

NICANOR PARRA
San Fabián de Alico, La Reina, Chile, 1914 – 2018 (not specified)

Black Dog at End of Poem

There are poems we read,
when we've had the good fortune of a modern education,

poems with discoveries like 'the crow's alabaster wing,'
not the poem we thought we were reading, another,
sliding, twisting, as from a major key to a minor.
And we follow. Not this book, another ...

But let me assure you,
even with good fortune,
with a hundred re-invented languages,
                              with six twists or twelve,

nothing will frighten the black dog when he comes.

PHILIPPE JACCOTTET
Moudon, Switzerland, 1925 –

From This, Poetry?

Rain. If not rain, fog.
As certain as a chrome door,
a Swarovski bracelet.

As Mafalda or Fatima
hauling blue trashbags
to the sidewalk on Wednesdays.

ANISE KOLTZ
Luxembourg, 1928 –

That Was

That was years ago, I think.
I was walking down some threadbare street,
it had rained, I'm sure of it.
A cabbie with a missing finger
crumpled his burger wrapper into a ball.

Nothing more. What city? What street?
The anaemic windows, the slurry lights,
the hundred others, also walking then.
That cabbie I can't forget.

REMCO CAMPERT
The Hague, 1929 –

Journey to the Antipodes

When we entered the first circle
we knew what to expect: ice, fog, hunger.
It was nothing like that.

By the fourth circle our sails hung limp,
we'd been swallowed by airlessness.

In our sweating ship our holy books
began to play tricks. Verses slipped about,
pages changed places, prayers
translated themselves into tongues.

We drank rain, we slid, inexorably, down the globe.

I'd lost count of the circles,
when at last! at last! the rats swarmed the gunwales,
plunged into the emerald sea.

And we saw the bright lip of land
and, calling to us, men
who'd lived here longer than the stones.

DAVID MALOUF
Brisbane, Queensland, Australia, 1934 –

Letter to Ovid, Tomis, 15 A.D.

Returning to rue Monsieur-le-Prince
I'll find nothing, of course. After all these years
I'll find the old couscous place boarded up.
Not likely! – more likely tarted up.
White tablecloths, not chequered to mask the spills,
the boss-cum-cook with his outsized moustache
shoved off to pasture in some rainy suburb,
or if he was unlucky, 'home,' as it's been called,
the hills behind Annaba (Hippo Regius to you)
or Algiers to have his throat slit
for being insufficiently of one side or the other.

It's not always good to go home.
I can attest to that.

They sang themselves through the night,
the men in the far block,
and were hanged in the morning,
one by one.

Inevitable night –
no moon, no star,
no comet, no cloud, no meteor,
no wind. No bird, no cricket,
no rat or worm, no twirling spider,
not anything.

The Scythians, however, only care for their sky …

You scurry down to the harbour,
the pebbly cove, that here passes for a harbour.
A Pontus trader has shown up.
Imperfect Greek, but intelligible,
and a Syrian hawking luxury,
Egyptian salt, oil, olives and lemons,
mullet sauce from Sardinia! and,
by way of Alexandria, Antioch
and unborn Constantinople,
threadbare gossip and
my letter, carried across two thousand years.

We're kin, you and I, it begins,
couldn't keep our mouths shut ...

Returning to rue Monsieur-le-Prince,
outside the old couscous place
I'll prefer, I think, not to be recognized.
I'll hang about a bit in the drizzle,
contemplate the new menu behind its glass.
No more Sidi Brahim, now Côte de something-or-other,
Château something-else.
A white taxi pulls up: two women in wobbly heels.
I wander down to the orientalist bookshop:
Has anything changed, after all these years,
of cuneiform, Linear A, Sanskrit?

I shake the drip from my umbrella,
old poems, Scythians, rain.

BREYTEN BREYTENBACH
Bonnievale, Western Cape, South Africa, 1939 –

Tonight, I Conquered

Do you remember, Bernd,
how you came to Las Palmas to say good-bye?
Well, it wasn't good-bye, not then, and not now.

I know why you came here, Bernd.
You didn't come to write poems.
This house, tonight, is too full for poems.

I know. I've come here many times myself,
not precisely this mountain, this village,
this house with its turquoise pool
and its lonely fig tree at the end of the garden.

I never sat behind that broad desk, and I never held that pen,
or that other instrument you have there in your hand.

But this place,
yes, this place I've been so many times it's almost a friend.

Bernd, in that cosy apartment overlooking the river
Loli and the girls are asleep, Natalia has a cold and is snoring.

It's only forty minutes, Bernd, the rain has stopped.
I promise you. When you arrive there'll be a poem waiting.

Tonight, I conquered, it will begin,
I stood alone and I conquered, vast empires,
                                    innumerable angels …

BERND DIETZ
Alcalá de Henares, Spain, 1953 –

Abraham, Truth Is

Also the snake between the stones,
the scorpion, the many-legged worm.

Yes, the cooing bird, the green tree,
red poppies in the meadow.

Yes, the bright lemon, jasmine,
the milky bride stepping from her bath.

Also the thorn and the blue thistle,
the ant, the clicking crab on the sand.

Ask your chiefs, your holy men,
also the repudiated wife, her children.

Ask your scrolls, your heavy books,
your copper-haloed saints flitting heavenward.

Also the shadow, the mirror.

BEJAN MATUR
Kahramanmaraş, Turkey, 1968 –

Death and His Kin

When Tal came home they were already waiting.
Two were on a street corner,
a fat one who held his arms wide
like the ex-weightlifter he was
and another of forgettable description
wearing a beige windbreaker, as this was December.
Two others jumped out of a white van, a Toyota.
They grabbed Tal by the collar, and shoved her inside.
Slut! hissed the one.
Whore! shouted the other.

We'll not talk about what went on between then and the trial.
Tal's father called on every friend and cousin,
and friend of friend of cousin and in-law,
Tal's mother made the rounds
of the usual ministries and police stations,
including the ones you cross the street not to see.
And always the answer was the same:
We've never heard of her.
Did she run away? Was she seeing a boy?
Don't be absurd!
We don't arrest children.

When Tal's case came to trial
the judge looked exactly as a judge should look.
That is to say, like her grandfather, and kindly.

And Death, when he came –
he stood on grand steps
surrounded by his generals and his kin.
And beneath an enormous portrait of himself,
he waved to the adoring crowd.

Tal al-Mallouhi
Damascus, 1991 – ?

Worms

I stared the worms,
down, down into their cold.

I stared the worms,
stared them down to their beginnings,
stared them cold.

I spoke the worms,
spoke back their pale insinuations.

No, no, I said.
Not yet, I said,
Not now.

This is a clump of earth,
this a shovel, and this bright air
and sky.

Worms! I said,

Not now.

Notes and Acknowledgements

The phrase "Strange Times, My Dear," which is used in the poem "Upside Down," is taken from the title of the *PEN Anthology of Contemporary Iranian Literature*. "Upside Down" is the title of a book by Eduardo Galeano, to whom this poem is dedicated.

I am grateful to the editors and publishers of the following magazines and books in which these poems appeared, some in different renditions:

Alba : "Worms"
The Antigonish Review: "Life Apologizes," "Self-portrait with Pines and Water"
Blue Tile: "A Book, the Wind," "De Falla at the Police Station"
Bridges: "A Large Man and His Shadow," "Arrival," "I'm Walking," "Man on Bridge"
Slush Pile Magazine: "The Bench Opposite"
Stand: "The Poet Descends, Willingly, the Stairs," "We Are Left, Gliding Away," "Woman at the Airport"

Special thanks to the staff at Guernica Editions, especially publishers Michael Mirolla and Connie McParland, and my very patient and precise editor, Elana Wolff.

I am also immensely grateful to Mark Frutkin, Alison Hobbs, Rebecca Leaver, Seymour Mayne, Richard Owens, and Susan Robertson, who have given so much of their time and themselves to read and listen to these poems, offering their thoughtful criticism, wisdom, hospitality, and friendship.

Maha Albari and Leonor Vulpe Albari, my debt to you through all these years, for your counsel and your patience especially, is immeasurable.

Cover art: "Abstract Black #17" by Leonor Vulpe Albari, courtesy of the artist.

The author acknowledges the support of the Ontario Arts Council and the City of Ottawa.

About the Author

Nicola Vulpe was born in Montreal but now lives in Ottawa, where he had studied literature before completing a doctorate in philosophy at the Sorbonne. He considers poetry an unfortunate habit, and doesn't get out much with the literati. He has nonetheless published two collections of poetry, *When the Mongols Return* and *Blue Tile*, a novella, *The Extraordinary Event of Pia H., who turned to admire a chicken on the Plaza Mayor*, and essays and articles on subjects as diverse as the twelfth tablet of the *Epic of Gilgamesh*, and the afterlife of Norman Bethune.

He likes to think that *Sealed in Struggle*, his anthology of Canadian poetry about the Spanish Civil War, contributed in a small way to patching up Hispano-Canadian relations after the brief and bloodless Turbot War of 1996, and that his article "The People with No Friends," published in *The Globe and Mail* at the start of the First Gulf War (Bush Sr.), helped draw world attention to the plight of the Kurds, and perhaps even helped save a few lives.

Printed in January 2019
by Gauvin Press,
Gatineau, Québec